Passport to Kabbalah

A Journey of Inner Transformation

Rabbi DovBer Pinson

SINAI LIVE BOOKS

Imprint of Rethink Partners, LLC

Rethink Partners books may be purchased for educational, business or sales promotional use. For more information please contact Rethink Partners, LLC at info@rethinkpartners.com.

ISBN-13: 978-0615625669 (Sinai Live Books)
ISBN-10: 0615625665

Rabbi Pinson is a world-renowned scholar, author, kabbalist and beloved spiritual teacher. He is a master of the revealed and inner aspects of Torah and has written dozens of groundbreaking books on Kabbalah and Philosophy.

Rabbi Pinson is the Rosh Yeshivah of the IYYUN Yeshivah and heads the IYYUN Center for Jewish Spirituality in Brooklyn, NY. He travels extensively and has attracted thousands of loyal followers and students around the world.

Learn more at www.iyyun.com.

Introduction

Life is a journey full of ups and downs, inside-outs, and unexpected detours. There are times when we think we know exactly where we want to be headed, and other times when we are so lost we don't even know where we are. Oftentimes, people get stuck in the idea of there being a pre-determined destination for this journey called life. They feel like they are supposed to be somewhere else, or they may feel like they will never get "there" — wherever "there" is.

Both of these perspectives take us out of the *eternal moment* of the here and now, the transcendent present of presence. But if we read deeply into the inner dimension of the Torah, we are able to see that the true test of life is not where you get to, but how you got there. The point of life is not only the destination one reaches, but also, the journey one embarks upon to get there.

Nowhere is this more evident than in the story of the patriarch Avraham / Abraham. Avraham first hears the Divine call impelling him to embark upon his spiritual journey with the cryptic words, *lech lecha*, "Go (to/for/by) yourself...to the land I will show you" (Bereishis, 12:1). There is much that is communicated by these two words, *lech lecha*. On first reading one can discern the implied meaning to "Go *to* yourself", suggesting that the journey is one of self-discovery, a kind of inner odyssey. From another perspective one can interpret these two words to mean, "Go *for* yourself", advocating a process of self-actualization — a taking control of, and responsibility for, one's own life path. And finally, a third understanding leads the reader to yet another teaching contained within these two words — that of "Going *by* Yourself". This final exegesis reveals the existential aspect of human nature, which is that ultimately we are all alone on this journey called life. We all have to figure it out for ourselves and be true to ourselves as we seek out and manifest our unique spark of Divinity in this beautiful, broken, and sometimes confusing world.

The Torah, and its vast body of inner explication, known as Kabbalah, is meant to aid and assist the honest and humble seeker of truth, peace, and happiness through the labyrinth of life in the most conscious, caring, and creative way possible. This ancient wisdom, reformulated into modern parlance, has proven itself over time to be functionally relevant for spiritually sensitive travelers along the path of self-refinement, reflection, and revelation.

The particular teachings collected here were transcribed from a series of informal interviews given in 2009. They are meant to introduce the reader to a number of key Kabbalistic concepts and to provide them with a series of accessible glimpses into various levels of expanded consciousness.

This book can be thought of as a kind of spiritual passport. Each short essay is another stamp to document a significant phase of the journey of awareness becoming aware of itself. As with a national passport book, these stamps are not meant to convey the entire depth or detail of a particular experience or destination, but are best utilized as a kind of recognized shorthand to chart the course of one's travels.

The interested reader may choose to engage this passport on a deeper level in order to project a potential future pathway, or to reflect upon meaningful sites and wonders previously encountered.

May these spiritual snapshots serve you well on your path, opening many doors, and allowing you access to experiences and realms of being hitherto beyond your imagination, beyond your limited self.

May you go in Peace and return in Peace.

– *Rav DovBer Pinson*

Self

Context vs. Content

For most of us, other people define who we are, and we are left to fill in the details. That is to say that for the most part, other people choose the *context* of our life, and we choose the *content*. The context can be thought of as "who we are", and our content is then "what or how we do."

For instance, you create a reality for yourself based on a certain belief system of who you are, or more likely, who you think you are supposed to be: "I am this person, I do these certain things, I don't do these other things," etc. Therefore, most of the choices you make in your life are merely selecting specific content from within the context of an externally imposed identity construct.

Let's say your parents, siblings, or educators have continuously told you: "You are not so smart, you are not such a good person." Slowly, you start believing these statements. You actually become that which others define you as. And then you make choices based on that definition. "I am not so smart," you tell yourself. "Maybe I'm not such a good person." The result is that you don't strive to act appropriately or to expand your mind.

But there is another way to live. You can create a life and identity for yourself wherein you are empowered to choose both your *context* and your *content*. In this way, you can decide "who you really are", and then fill in the "content" from that place.

Transform Your Life

Genuine transformation is about redirecting your consciousness. Seen in a certain way, it is really not a long drawn out process. Transformation can occur in a single moment. That moment is a sudden shift of consciousness. Instead of thinking of yourself as one way — and therefore struggling in or against that way — think of yourself as being completely different. Perceive of yourself as being totally beyond and above your problems.

It is much more psychologically productive to see yourself as a 'perfect' person, and thereby to aspire to live up to that image, than to see yourself as a negative person and perpetually struggle with that image.

This may sound overly simplistic. But deep down, everyone knows what this means. We all have our moments when we feel the most alive and most real and true to ourselves, when we are able to recognize our untainted 'inner perfection.' Imagine that powerful person is who you really are at all times and make your choices based on that perspective. When you lose your connection to this reality inside yourself, stop, take a deep breath and redirect your energy and awareness towards manifesting the Real You.

You will find a lot of things that bother you when you are in a narrow place of constricted consciousness simply stop bothering you when you are able to access a more expansive place within yourself. You are no longer full of anger, jealousy, or resentments. All of a sudden you are beyond the minutiae of petty concerns, you are larger than the story attached to your temporary suffering. It is a choice you can make. Are you going to buy into the higher, more expansive story, or the lower, constricted story? This is the shift.

How do you do it? By declaring and believing the declaration that, "I really am a better person. I am more than my momentary emotions and lapses of larger perspective. I am free to choose my path and responsible for co-creating my own reality and identity."

Visualize yourself above your problems. Visualize yourself as the most perfect, elevated, open person in the world. Visualize yourself as that person and then make choices from that place. Create this higher, expansive context for your life and all the details and content will be filled in accordingly. Shift happens, and it happens in one moment.

Journey

Wants Vs. Needs

Typically, a "want" or craving arises when there is a perceived emptiness, a feeling of something missing or out of alignment. Therefore, awareness of your ego's appetites is therefore an effective indicator about what is really going on in your life beneath the surface. Examining your unconscious, reflexive desires allows you to get a glimpse into your deeper self, showing you what aspect or area has to be filled or addressed.

Let's explore this a little deeper.

There is a teaching in *Pirkei Avos*, The Ethics of Our Fathers, that says, "Nullify your will for the divine will. Make your will as the divine will." These two statements refer to two progressive stages.

The first stage is nullifying your personal will for something higher. This entails a redirection of your internal compass towards healing, growth, discipline, love, responsibility, and compassion; a return to the world of *Yichud*, or "Unity." A commitment to these noble ideals will move you out of the box of your ego's quest for self-centered instant gratification. It is only when you make space within yourself that you are able to sensitize yourself to the needs of another. This 'other' could come in the form of a friend, an enemy, the environment, or your Creator.

After you have purified and refined your relationship to your own will and desires, the next stage occurs when your desire actually becomes an expression of the Divine Desire. When you have reached this point, you are no longer subduing your natural inclination for base and temporal appetites, but your will has actually been transformed and now desires those higher ideals that were once seen as separate from your own intuitive appetites.

Let's make this simple:

Imagine you want something. You have to ask yourself a series of questions: "I want this thing. Is it good for me physically, mentally, emotionally, and spiritually? Or is it bad for me? Is getting this thing going to advance my emotional/mental/spiritual development or is it going to hinder it? Will the satisfaction of this desire put me two steps forward or two steps back from where I want to be?"

Most of the time we are *subjective* beings and we can, therefore justify just about anything. We can almost always give ourselves a good excuse to convince ourselves that we need some particular thing or experience, whether its positive or negative.

To untangle ourselves from this subjectivity in order to respond from a more objective and clear-headed space, the first step is to strip away any sense of perceived pleasure you would receive from the object or experience. Try to see the desire from an objective perspective, unrelated to your self.

That is to say that, if you want something but are unsure if you should pursue it, you should strip away the subjective pleasure that you would receive from it and try to become an objective observer. This is stage one. What you are really doing at this point is attempting to nullify your desire. You are saying to yourself, "I want to know if this is the correct thing for me to do or not."

One method of stripping away your sense of personal pleasure is be to imagine that you are giving advice to another person regarding the very same issue. Since you have no personal gain in the situation, what would you tell another person to do? Would you tell them to pursue or refrain from this desire? Whatever you would tell another person to do, do yourself.

The next step after perceiving your desire objectively would be to say, "Okay, maybe I actually should get or do this particular thing because it really is the right thing for me to do objectively, and now I desire it again." Now your desire is an expression of a divine desire. This is a higher level of awareness, wherein one's desire has been refined and reflected upon.

In summary, the first stage is the subjugation of your initial desire, stripping the raw desire of any sense of anticipated gratification. The second stage is the elevation and reintegration of your desire. This second stage is not about living less, or limiting yourself (as on the first stage), but about living more — more consciously, more creatively, and more compassionately. This includes compassion for others — taking into account how your actions affect those whom you love or those around you — as well as compassion for yourself — taking into account how this particular action may affect your own development, progress, and enjoyment of life beyond the immediate moment.

When you unconsciously follow your whims and desires you are inevitably pursuing a façade, a mirage. This is otherwise referred to as "chasing the wind." The higher aspect of desire is activated when you are able to approach a situation from a place of objectivity and then to *reengage* the experience from a place of subjectivity in order to fully enjoy it.

It is one thing to say to yourself: "I am stripping away my desires. I am abolishing my attachment to my appetites. I am just going to eat to stay alive. I am not seeking any pleasure from the experience.

It is irrelevant to me if the food is good or bad."
But that is not the deepest level of living because
you are not fully participating in the experience on
all levels of your being. Fully participating in the
experience would lead one to say: "I need to eat
because I am hungry and I want to stay alive. But
I am also going to engage my refined and reflected
upon desire and look at this fruit and say: "Wow,
what a beautiful fruit! And it tastes delicious!" Now
your desires are perfect expressions of the Divine
desire. Now the physical act of eating is a spiritual
activity that connects your soul to the Source of the
food.

Journey

No Coincidences

There is no such thing as mere coincidence, or happenstance. Everything is a manifestation of the Light of the Creator. The One Light is being revealed in many vessels. Everything is interconnected, and everything in life has meaning and purpose.

But just because everything has purpose does not mean that we always understand its meaning. For instance: A single guy synchronistically meets an intriguing woman and says, "This is heavenly decreed. I have to marry this person." This is not necessarily so. Just because you see the coherence of events leading up to meeting this person, does not mean that you have to follow them out, or pursue the relationship. Perhaps, you were introduced to this person for the purpose of being shown what you should become more acutely aware of, and what you should not pursue.

Your first reaction should be to ask yourself: "What does this experience mean to me? Is this supposed to open me up to new possibilities, or is this supposed to strengthen my discipline and commitment to that which I am currently involved in? Am I supposed to resist this or receive it?"

How does one know whether they should receive,

pursue, resist, or refrain from an encounter or experience? This is precisely where the previously mentioned practice of stripping away your sense of perceived personal pleasure would be an effective tool. As explored earlier regarding wants, desires, and needs — try to make the issue an 'objective' issue, and then determine if there is a divine desire to either receive or resist it.

Every experience in life has meaning. But not every experience is meant to be pursued. Sometimes things that are shown to us are challenges and we are meant to overcome them. But everything has a purpose. Everything is telling and teaching us something. Every encounter and experience can be our teacher, teaching us who we truly are in the present moment, and forcing us to ask ourselves the important questions.

Finding Purpose

In life there is always a larger purpose, which is the over-arching theme of your ultimate trajectory and journey. This meta-narrative poses the questions: "Where am I headed? What is my purpose?" But there is also the plethora of smaller "purposes" in each of our day-to-day lives.

We all seek to answer the ever-looming question of our general purpose of life, but sometimes to see the bigger picture we need to find meaning and purpose in the smaller details of life.

When you only think about the larger picture, it is sometimes hard to see where your life is headed. In Kabbalistic terminology, your life's meaning and purpose is like the Light. Then there are the small day-to-day things and situations in your life that are the Vessels, the containers that receive, reflect, and refract the larger Light.

Certain events or experiences in life may seem trivial and purposeless. When this happens, you are perceiving more of the *vessel* of a situation. Everything has both an aspect of light (meaning, purpose, connection) and an aspect of vessel (lack of meaning, purposelessness, separation).

When you perceive things in your life as having meaning or some kind of connection to something greater, you are starting to see the Light. The more meaning you perceive, the more transparent the experience becomes, and the more interaction you can have with the depth of the experience. The more Light, the less vessel — the less blockage.

Paradoxically, when seeking out meaning and purpose in life, it is more important to focus on the small details. These are the many vessels that receive and express the One Light. Instead of always fixating on the grand arc or theme of your life, which you do have and can always access on some level of your consciousness, it is imperative to locate the Light present within the vessels in your life. This is like the impossibility of staring directly at the sun.

In fact, it is more beautiful and revealing to be able to get a glimpse of the individual rays of the sun as they illuminate a particular locality or stretch of land. This same dynamic also gives a sense of majesty, mystery, and poetry to a rainbow — truly a refraction of the One Light into a multitude of interpenetrating prisms and vessels which come together to create something greater than the sum of their parts.

The reason why most people do not find the larger purpose in their lives is because they are stuck in the details. When you are stuck, you are only seeing the vessel. This often leads you to ask things like, "Why does this thing always happen to me? Why am I in this relationship? Why can't I make money?" The problem is, these questions are not followed to their fullest expression — which would reveal the Light and purpose behind their appearance. You are stuck in how the Light is presented to you, which is the vessel.

What you should really be trying to do is to go deeper into the details in order to penetrate the vessel to locate the Light, the meaning, and the purpose hiding beneath the surface. Instead of looking for the huge, great purpose of your life, try instead to focus on and find the small purposes in your life. "What does this particular thing mean to me? How can I learn from this experience? Why does this pattern engage me? How can this opportunity create a better life and sense of self for me?"

By breaking down and building on the smaller purposes in your life, you are actually doing the necessary work to deconstruct the larger vessel that conceals the One Light. Through breaking the larger vessel, the greater Light will be revealed to you. Finding your overall purpose comes through realizing your smaller purposes.

Details, which contain the secrets to our smaller purposes, allow us to see the bigger picture. In life, your purpose is constantly evolving. There is an over-arching purpose, but the day-to-day life revealing itself right now must be in touch with its own potentials and purposes in order to receive the One Light of our Lives as it is unfolding before our very eyes.

Self Esteem

Healthy self-esteem requires a balance between the 'attribute' of *Netzach* or "Self-Confidence", and the 'attribute' of *Hod* or "Humility." Unbridled self-confidence can lead to arrogance, and extreme humility can lead to a disempowered feeling of being unworthy. Self-confidence comes from the awareness that we are special and have something distinct to contribute. Humility comes from the awareness that others do too.

The aspect of Netzach comes from tapping into our inner Perfection. The aspect of Hod comes from tapping into our inner Imperfection. There is a dimension of self that is always pure, strong, true, and noble. There is also another dimension of self that constantly struggles with obstacles, challenges, lack, and deficiency. There is the inner struggler, the divine Wrestler, and there is the inner perfect one, the Tzaddik.

We are all unique. Not everyone is alike. In fact, we are not supposed to be alike. Just because someone has a certain difference, or particular way of doing things, does not mean that they are wrong. Maybe they do not fit in because they have a certain way of speaking, laughing, or completing a task. We must all strive to understand that part of this wonderful universe is that the Infinite One desires to be expressed in many finite vessels. Every person is a one-of-a-kind vessel, an exclusive expression.

The basic understanding that we all need to realize, about ourselves and about each other, is that maybe we are not all supposed to be the same. Be yourself. That is why the Creator created *you*.

Daily Life

To live fully we need to be open to all kinds of experience. In life, a lot of opportunities and occasions are presented to us throughout the day or throughout our lives. We may not actually be equipped to handle certain events, and in fact, we don't really want them to happen to us. There can arise a certain sense of resistance to unexpected occurrences: "I don't want this to happen. This cannot be true." There is a certain sense of denial in this response.

The first step of opening up to experience is to simply accept whatever it is as a truth in your life. "This is something that is real and I am really experiencing it right now. I am going to be present with this experience." Being present with an experience will allow you to start seeing some semblance of meaning within it.

So instead of resisting whatever it is that you are experiencing and saying, "This cannot be true, it is not real." Or, "This can't be happening to me." Try simply being with what is. Often just being with the experience and saying, "This is really real, I actually am feeling this," can allow us to get something out of the experience we may not otherwise have gotten. This can come in the form of a realization, an inspiration, or a blessing.

Any experience, even if it is a negative experience, can be redemptive in some unexpected way. Let's say, for instance, you are feeling sad. Do not deny that you are feeling sad. Just acknowledge that you are feeling the sensation of sadness. Once you acknowledge what you are experiencing, that in itself is already penetrating the density of the vessel of the experience in order to locate the Light within the perceived darkness.

Remember, you are not shutting yourself off from life. You are opening yourself up to experience. That in itself will allow you to find and create meaning within the context of any particular experience.

Free Will

There are multiple levels of being:

1) One level of being is where you have a lower level of free choice, in which you are operating outside of a context of Divine orchestration. From this perspective you would say, "I am the creator of my own existence." This is a perspective of pure freewill.

2) Then you may move into a higher/deeper consciousness in which you are no longer an independent being that is creating your own life, but you are actually an extension or manifestation of a greater being through which your life is being manifest. This is a perspective of pure non-dual Divine Providence.

3) Finally, there is something beyond both perspectives, a third level, where you are so connected with the Source of life, that you are both a creation and co-creator of your existence. Your individual choices are actually one with the divine choice. When you make a choice ask yourself, "Who is making this choice?" The answer, from this level of consciousness, is that you and the Creator are making the choice together, as it were, because you are so in sync with the reality of existence.

The lowest level of free choice is only 'content' based (as mentioned previously). For instance, when you are hungry, you can ask: "Should I have a sandwich or a slice of pizza?" That is not a real choice on the level of 'context'. The deepest level of free choice is to choose 'who you are', not just 'what you want', and for that choice to be sync with the Creator's image of who you should be. That is really the essence of free choice. It is both a real free choice and it was meant to be.

Everything that occurs in life, once it happens already, is meant to be. How do we know that it was meant to be? — Because it happened. Once something happens, that was what was intended to happen. Everything. Even the negative experiences, or what we interpret to be negative experiences, were meant to be. If it happened, it was meant to be.

There are three levels of existence:

1) Lower Unity, referred to as *Yesh* or "Existence", where there is *Bechirah* or "Choice".

2) Higher Unity, referred to as *Ayin* or "Nothingness", where all that exists is Hashem's *Yediah*, Divine Awareness. This is a level of no independent free choice.

3) Ultimate unity, referred to as *Etzem* or "Essence", where both *yesh* and *ayin* are paradoxical but

interpenetrating perspectives. In this place both levels are true, and our choices are in harmony with the will of the Creator.

So from the deepest perspective, we look back into the past and say, "Everything in my life up to this point was meant to be, even the negative things. And now that I know it was all meant to be, whether positive or negative, what can I learn from it, and how do I best utilize my free will in the present moment in order to create a brighter future from that providential past?"

Reincarnation

There are two levels of self:

1) The context or backdrop, the experiencer.

And

2) The content or storyline, the actual experiences.

The lower level of self is our *autobiographical self*. This is the self that you know — the certain ways that you think, feel, and interact with others. This is generally what you think of when you think of your 'self'. This is the level of self you are referring to when you say, "I know myself." What you are really saying is that you know your story.

Every person has his or her own story. When a person is born, they are born with a particular soul type — an individual soul. Imagine there is a blank sheet of paper. That is the content of your character and consciousness at the beginning of your life. It is empty. But this blank sheet of paper already has a hue, a shade, a texture, an imprint. One sheet of paper has the hue of red; another has the hue of blue, and another green. One paper has a rough texture, and another is smooth.

Let's imagine it this way. A person has a natural inclination. Even before they write anything of their story, meaning before they have any experience in life, there is already this or that inclination that is part of their makeup, so to speak; their spiritual DNA. It is their natural disposition for a certain way of being. One person is inclined to be open and giving, and another person is inclined to be harsh and restrained. This is a result of the particular 'coloring' that will inform how their story unfolds and how it is understood.

Then you write your story. Day one, day two, everyone is writing their own story. Everyone is an infant and eventually grows up. We are all having our own unique experiences. The experiences that we are having are imprinted on the backdrop of our paper — the paper that already has a coloring. So you can read the same story on day one and day two according to two different people. But the way that person number one (whose blank paper was red) and person number two (whose paper was originally blue), experience the same exact event is going to be expressed and interpreted differently. They are both eating and they are both sleeping, but they are experiencing it differently.

Then we continue with our lives and we write a full narrative. So we may ask ourselves at any point in life, "Who am I?" We are actually the story that we have written up until that moment. That is who we are. We are the authors of our lives. We are writing our book, the book of life — our book of life. This is our individual story.

But we must remember that we are also informed by the original hue and texture of the blank slate that was our soul before birth. That is not to say that we are totally fixed as unchanging archetypes. We all have the capability of transforming ourselves and moving beyond our initial inclinations through the hard work of self-reflection and refinement. Therefore we can ask ourselves, "Why or how did my blank sheet of paper get colored in such a way?"

This is where the concept of reincarnation comes in. On a conscious level, we do not remember our past lives, because we were not there — at least consciously. If your previous life was written upon a red sheet of paper, and your current life is being written on a blue sheet of paper, then you are now the blue soul. In all likelihood you will not remember your red life, because consciously you were not there.

There is a relationship between the blue life and the red life, of course. The way it manifests is that the things that were worked on by person number one in their red life, those are the things that come easy for person number two in their blue life.

Person number one worked on anger during their lifetime. They overcame the emotion of anger, and therefore person number two has no trouble with anger. They might struggle with other things, but not anger. We are speaking of person number one and person number two, but they are really the same soul manifest in two different lives — the same sheet of paper with two different hues and textures and two different stories being written that are all really part of one story — a past life and a current life.

Each successive incarnation we are attempting to live out another color and quality until we complete the spectrum and live a full life. So on one level we are completely given a blank slate at the beginning of life and we are pure. Like the morning blessing goes, "The soul that You give me is pure." It is full of infinite potential. And yet it is linked to a past life and a future life.

There can sometimes be a connection between your past life and your future life. If in this present life you are working on something — you are trying to accomplish something and it is not working out — it is possible for your previous soul, which is still part of your root-soul, to be impregnated into your current soul for a period of time in order to give you an extra spiritual boost of energy so you can overcome certain obstacles and achieve your *tikkun*. This 'impregnation' is referred to as *ibbur*.

The idea of reincarnation and individual immortality are not mutually exclusive. You do exist eternally, and yet aspects of your self, which were not developed or refined in this life, will be articulated in your next life.

The real meaning of a Soul Mate goes back to the birth of our Soul-Root. When a Soul is created, at its root, it has a male and female aspect within it. As it says in the Torah about the creation of the first human being, "Male and Female He created them." So too with all root-souls — they possess both a masculine and feminine counterpart. These are two halves that make up a whole Soul. Your true Soul Mate is the other half of your Root-Soul that you have been separated from since birth. You actually are supposed to marry this same soul in each successive incarnation. This is your ultimate Soul Mate.

Finding God

Not every person experiences G-d the same way. Some people can find G-d sitting at the beach during sunset. For some people that experience does nothing. Some people find G-d through a text. Some people find G-d in love. Some people find G-d in awe, and some in prayer. The first question in finding G-d should be: "How do I find myself? What makes me feel most alive? What makes me feel most connected?" Then deepen that experience, go into it, follow it all the way to its Source.

If you feel you are an artistic person, then maybe you will find G-d through art. If you are a musical person, then maybe you will find G-d through music. If you are a physical person, then maybe you will find G-d through dance or movement. If you are a very textual based person, then maybe find G-d through study. Your experience has to be consistent with who you are.

There is no one way to find G-d. Every person has his or her own way, and that way is distinct and unique to them.

Remember, as mentioned previously, when Avraham first heard the Divine call beckoning him to embark upon his journey, he heard the words, *lech lecha,* "Go *to* or *for* yourself". But Avraham also understood that going *to* or *for* yourself necessitated a form of "going *by* yourself". He needed to find his own way. No two souls are identical, and each of us needs to find our own path.

Certainly, it is beneficial to find a supportive community of like-minded people, a spiritual home where you feel welcomed and recognized for who you are. When you are surrounded by others who value your journey, you will be encouraged to pursue this path of self-realization. But always remember that finding your own way is essentially a private and personal experience — you have to find it wherever it is that *you* find it.

Simple Prayer

The dynamics of prayer have multiple levels. Prayer can be a petition, where you are asking for something. Prayer can be a connection, where you are reaching out to connect with something larger than yourself. Prayer can be praise, where you are swept away by a sense of awe and gratitude, and you just want to sing praises to the Creator.

One interesting thing about prayer is that if you want to make your prayers more meaningful, you have to eventually surrender all your 'understandings' about prayer. This means that when you pray, you should pray like a child. You can be very complex and interesting when you are trying to prepare for, or understand things. But that should all be prior to the actual act of prayer. Once you begin to pray, there should be a sense of simplicity in your prayer. Think to yourself that you are just connecting, even if you don't understand why or how.

There is an image that I have one of my children. He walks into a room and just says, "*Tati.*" I turn to him and say, "What do you want?" And he does not say anything. He just turns around and walks out of the room. I realize that this is like prayer. My child did not want anything from me. He just wanted to know that I was there. This is prayer.

There is a certain sense in which I just want to know. Knowing can be a very simple thing. Like a child, we just want to know that we are protected and that Someone is there.

Prayer is calling out to G-d and knowing that G-d is there. All the complexities and intricacies of prayer are things to wrestle with either before or after prayer. There is a Kabbalistic teaching that says, "I pray like a child." To pray like a child is very simple. Just say the words. The early spiritual masters offer voluminous instructions and intentions to aid in prayer and mediation. They would take one word and look at the numeric value of that word in order to penetrate to its core and to associate it with other similar words or numbers or symbols. They would teach a litany of specific concepts that you should focus on as you are reading the Hebrew. They would instruct how to meditate when you would say G-d's name — what it means and represents.

These are very complex systems of prayer. You can literally pray with these *kavanos* or intentions for multiple hours. Then the Baal Shem Tov came along and said, "just pray with the words." That's it. The intentions are the words themselves. Not even the meaning of the words, just the letters. Hold onto the *Aleph*, for example. On a certain level, it does not matter what it means. The letters contain the Light. This is the true simplicity of prayer and it is very deep. In a way it is very simple, and in a way, it is actually deeper than all the complex systems and structures applied by the sophisticated intellect.

Elevated Prayer

There is a Kabbalistic meditation to help you get into your prayers, wherein you imagine yourself praying in the presence of righteous people in Gan Eden. It might be difficult for you to imagine this. If so, imagine yourself praying in the presence of the people you love most and feel secure with. This opens you up to prayer because it allows you to feel very protected. You feel complete and wholesome in the presence of your loved ones or idealized *tzaddikim*.

This is a good visualization to actually get yourself into the state of prayer. Maybe you are in a community and you do not feel so comfortable with the person next to you, or just in general. Maybe the person is making noise, or there are other distracting noises in the space. Imagine yourself sitting with the best company possible. You are just sitting there. All you want to say is "Father," that's it. This is a very simple practice of prayer. Of course, it can get much more complicated. You can have extremely complex and in-depth meditations before, during, and after prayer.

In the Talmud, when it speaks about a group of sages called the "early pious ones". It says they would 'wait for an hour' before they prayed. What is this idea of waiting?

There is an interesting debate between some Talmudic scholars, Maimonides and others, about what this means? Did it mean that they would settle and empty their minds of all thoughts? Or would they empty their minds of the thoughts they had before, and then enter into new thoughts, or new state of consciousness? Would they approach prayer in a state of emptiness, or would they refill their consciousness with holy or refined thoughts before prayer?

Maimonides is of the opinion that they would settle their minds. They would empty and clear their minds. There are many Kabbalistic techniques to quiet your mind. The simplest technique is to just observe your mind. This is a practice called *Habatah*, which means, "to observe yourself." Just close your eyes and watch your thoughts arise and fall. When you watch your thoughts rising, instead of allowing them to overflow your mind, just observe them going up and down. In so doing, you are actually allowing your mind to settle, and as a result, your mind slows down. Without judgment, and certainly without resistance, just observe your thoughts without pushing them aside. Allow the thoughts to naturally rise and fall, allowing your mind to settle.

Another way to settle the mind is to select a focal point that you keep bringing your attention back to. For example, this could be your breath or a very simple idea or abstract image in your mind. This allows your mind to settle, as well as activating it on certain levels through intense concentration. You can practice this for any amount of time to help settle and enliven your mind, and then you can properly engage in prayer.

Or, instead of settling the mind, you can choose to fill your mind with appropriate thoughts for prayer and meditation. To do this, you can introduce a whole complex system of new thoughts. For instance, instead of thinking about your everyday life, think about the *merkavah*, the Kabbalistic chariot that carries one beyond this world, *the beis hamikdash,* the holy temple in all its details, or the interconnection between multiple universes.

The Morning Prayer is divided into four sections, which parallel the Four Inner Worlds. Through the process of the morning prayers you are moving from a functional and body-centered place, to an emotional and heart-centered place, to an intellectual and mind oriented place, to a transcendent space of soul and spirituality. These are four parallel universes. If you can get inside the system and understand how it works within you, you can be much more present within your own body, emotions, mind, and soul.

You are then actually following the path of prayer. You are transcending and including your entire self. You are not leaving your body in one place and your emotions in another place. You are engaging the whole self. You are acknowledging that the body is a vessel, a holy vessel. Then you are moving to a higher place and engaging your emotions, then your mind, and finally you come to the infinitesimal point of transcendence.

Incidentally, or interestingly enough, the peak of the prayer experience comes during *tachanun* when you start praying for others. At this point there is a complete transcendence of self and you are no longer saying that, "I have done something," but that, "we have done something." You are asking for forgiveness for the sins and mistakes of the entire community. You are effectively identifying with "the people", rather than just with your ego-self. This is the ultimate level of transcendence, which is beyond self, while still including self. There is a 'you', and you are praying, but you are praying for the collective. This is a more holistic and involved level of prayer, which is more expansive and more engaged.

Journey

Mystical Experience Through Study

Delving deeply into a sacred text is one of the most mystical and spiritual experiences that you can have. When you are really able to penetrate and animate a text, that text becomes alive and revealed.

By themselves, letters and words printed on a page are dead. Essentially they have no meaning. That is the definition of a pure vessel — there is no light. Then you, the reader, come along and infuse the words with meaning and all of a sudden, the text comes to life. When you break open that vessel, a flood of light can be revealed through the text. This is one of the deepest spiritual experiences available. That is why serious Torah study is not only an intellectual exercise, relegated to the linear, logical, left side of the brain. To be sure, it is an intellectual avenue or endeavor, but some people mistake it for being only about the intellect. But truthfully, it is not just about the intellect. It is about the intellect connecting us to the Creator and to Creation through the creative application of our focused consciousness. This is the ultimate experience of deep, spiritual study — when you can break open the vessel and bask in a river of Light.

In the experience of serious study, there is a right-brain experience and a left-brain experience. You start off with the left-brain, very analytical and aware of your separate sense of self. But as you delve deeper into the text, there has to be a moment where you stop being just yourself, separate and defined.

There was a profound Chassidic teacher that was once teaching in public. All of a sudden he just stopped and left the room. His disciples asked him, "Why did you stop?" He replied to them that it was the first time he was teaching and actually heard himself speak. This means that because he was such a deep teacher, when he would start to teach he would get so into the teachings, that there would be a complete loss of self. He was just revealing — it was actually revelation. His ego, or separate sense of self, ceased to be a filter for the Living Word. He was receiving. That is the deepest experience.

In the beginning of study, you are using the left side of the brain and then all of a sudden, something just opens you up to the right side of the brain. Now something beyond your brain is flowing through you. It is revealing Torah. That is a very deep level of experience.

Becoming a Vessel for the Miraculous

There are three steps in the process of becoming a vessel for the miraculous. They are: Speaking, Visualizing, Surrendering.

Speaking:

The first step is speaking about, giving voice to, and articulating what you want. Through language, we are able to bring to consciousness and clarity that which we seek to work on or work towards.

The liberatory process of becoming free from the bondage of Egypt did not begin until the people "cried out", and only then did G-d hear their prayers. As it is written, "And they groaned…and G-d heard their groan…" (Shemos, 2:23-24).

The Israelites were slaves for over two hundreds years, but because there was no movement or opening on the part of the people, there was, as it were, no opening from Above. This is alluded to in the well known dictum that, "The Above mirrors the below." Until the people spoke to G-d, G-d did not speak to the people.

The moment the people cried out, this initiated an opening from below, and there was then a corresponding movement and opening from Above. The people cried and G-d listened.

We need to open up to G-d regarding the issues that are bothering us. Speak to the Creator as you would speak to your closest, most beloved, non-judgmental friend. Say everything that is hurting you. Speak about all your inner constrictions and limitations. Verbally declare: "G-d, this is no good. I need Your help. This is not working. Please comfort, guide, strengthen, and inspire me to rise to the challenges in my life and become who I came here to be."

Visualization:

The next stage is to visualize the reality you wish to create for yourself. Attempt to generate as detailed an image of that potential future reality as you can in your mind's eye. Hold that image. Enter into it. Explore its inner chambers and intricate passageways. See it. Hear it. Smell it. Touch it. Be it.

The first stage, speaking, is a reflective stage, wherein you look inwards in order to acknowledge and identify your problem areas and opportunities for growth. This second stage, visualization, is a practice in creative projection. Visualize success. Imagine enlightenment. Dream lucidly about your deepest aspirations.

Surrendering:

The third, very important stage is the stage of surrender and acceptance of what is and what will be. This process is a bit of a paradox. First you say what is bothering you, then you imagine a rectified reality, and now you are surrendering to a state of *Ayin*, "No-thing-ness". What's the logic in this?

The truth is, we cannot allow a miracle to occur if we still want to remain in control or in charge of our limited sphere of reality. Once we are able to admit our ultimate powerlessness in the presence of the Infinite One who moves and molds all worlds, then we are able to open ourselves up to a potential miracle in our lives, something bigger than and beyond ourselves manifesting itself before our very eyes.

As the Psalmist says, "I lift up my eyes to the mountains, and ask, *me'ayin ya'voh ezri*, 'from where will my salvation come'? My salvation comes from the Creator of the heaven and earth" (Psalms, 121:1-2). Most often this passage is read as a question and answer: Where will my help come from? And the answer is: From the Creator of heaven and earth.

But on a deeper level, the question, *me'ayin ya'voh ezri*, "from where will come my salvation?" becomes a statement: It is specifically *me'ayin*, 'from

51

the place of no-thing-ness', that my salvation will come.

In order to become a vehicle for the miraculous in your life to manifest a new reality for yourself, you first have to enter into the limitless place of *ayin* or "no-thing-ness", in order to empty yourself of the old reality. This is called, "The nullification of the separate I, or ego." When a person lives humbly, with a measure of surrender, they may say to themselves, "This is what my situation is, this is what was given to me, and I accept it."

On one level, they are practicing a nullification of the expectations of their ego. If a person comes from a place of *ayin*, they can create a new *yesh* or "sense of being", a new form, a new reality for themselves.

Ayin is the place of no-thing-ness and pure potential, the formlessness that precedes the creation of a particular form or *Yesh*, the some-thing-ness. When a person humbles himself, through extreme self-sacrifice, he becomes the embodiment of *Ayin*. He is then able to enter into the silence that comes before the sound, the stillness that is before the next cycle, the emptiness that exists before the future fullness, and it is through entering into and becoming *ayin* that he is able to be the instrument and medium through which the new flow of blessings can be revealed.

On a physical plane, where the physical mirrors the spiritual, if there is a desire to alter or change an image or form, the way to do it is to first un-create that shape, and then to shape a new one. For instance, let's say you want to change a silver cup to a silver plate. First you need to flatten out the old form and then you can create the new one.

On a spiritual level, it works much the same. To alter reality, to transform that which is, one needs to dissolve or neutralize the object, subject, or issue to the state of limitless potential — *Ayin*. And only then can a new arrangement of reality become manifest.

If you consider the internal mechanics of the act of prayer, which is traditionally where miracles are initiated or encountered, you are really doing two things. On one hand, you are completely surrendering to life the way it is. For example: Let's say someone is sick, heaven forbid. In prayer, you are saying, "I understand this person is sick because that is Your will G-d, and I completely accept that." This is a nullification of self. You are nullifying your will and desire for the Creator's will and desire. Your ego wants or expects one thing, but maybe this reality as it is, is what the Creator wants, and you humbly accept that. This is a condition of *ayin*.

But simultaneously you are also saying, "Please G-d change Your will." What you are doing here is moving from a place of *ayin* (nothingness) to a state of *yesh* (some-thing-ness). The *ayin* is an acceptance stage; the *yesh* is an assertion stage. In prayer you are simultaneously saying, "I accept this person as sick and yet I am praying for this person to be well." Prayer is an expression that asserts your understanding that on one level, creation is perfect because it is the will of G-d, the design of the Creator. Yet you are also communicating your desire to go back into the *ayin* place of infinite potential and recreate a new existence, a new *yesh*.

This dynamic is expressed in the traditional movement of swaying back and forth during prayer. This is called "*shokeling*", a constant motion back and forth. Symbolically, the idea of moving constantly back and forth represents both of these ideas — *yesh and ayin.*

When you move in, you are bowing in a submissive posture. You are saying, "I accept things the way they are." But when you pull your head back in a more confrontational posture, you are saying, "I do not accept things the way they are. I am suggesting they should be different."

Prayer is about both acceptance and non-acceptance. Because if it just about acceptance, then everything is perfect and there is nothing to strive for, nothing to ask for. But if everything is about perpetual struggle, then you are constantly frustrated.

The ideal balance is between *yesh* and *ayin*. If we can balance these two states, then we can create miracles in our lives. This is not just theoretical. This balance must actually be lived. If we can live in the balance between fullness and emptiness, between *yesh* and *ayin*, then we can enter into a place of emptiness and infinite potential in order to emerge and open up to a miracle, a new form or manifestation of our life.

About
Rav DovBer Pinson

Rav DovBer Pinson is a world-renowned scholar, author, and kabbalists. He is recognized as one of the world's foremost authorities on authentic Kabbalah and Judaic philosophy. Rav Pinson is a beloved spiritual teacher and mentor to many. Through his books, lectures, seminars and consul he has touched and inspired the lives of tens of thousands the world over.

Among his published works are:

- *Reincarnation & Judaism; The Journey of the Soul*
- *Inner Rhythms; The Kabbalah of Music*
- *Meditation & Judaism; Jewish Meditative Paths*
- *Toward the Infinite*
- *Jewish Wisdom on the Afterlife: The Mysteries, the Myths, & the Meanings*
- *Upsherin; A Boys First Hair Cut*
- *Tefilin: A Guide & Deeper Exploration of Tefilin*
- *Thirty-Two Gates of Wisdom; Awakening through Kabbalah*
- *Eight Lights; 8 Meditations for Chanukah*
- *The Purim Reader: The Holiday of Purim Explored*

- *The IYYUN Hagadah: The Hagadah Companion*
- *Reclaiming the Self: The Way of Teshuvah*
- *The Garden of Paradox: The Essence of Non-Dualism*

Rav DovBer Pinson is the Rosh Yeshiva of the IYYUN Yeshiva and heads IYYUN Center in Brownstone Brooklyn.
www.IYYUN.com

About Sinai Live Books

 Sinai Live is committed to assisting high-quality teachers share their wisdom. Our goal is to enhance our readers' personal Jewish journeys and elevate everyday life through thoughtful and insightful content. We aim to engage, inspire and encourage further exploration.

Our books include:

Telushkinisms: Wisdom to the Point
by Rabbi Joseph Telushkin

Footsteps: Perspectives for Daily Life
by Rebbetzin Esther Jungreis

Insights: Concise and Thoughtful Jewish Wisdom
by Rabbi Benjamin Blech

More Precious Than Pearls: A Prayer for the Women of Valor in Our Lives
edited by Mark B. Pearlman

Visit www.sinailive.com or contact us at info@ sinailive.com to learn more.

About Rethink Partners

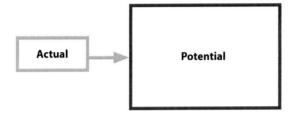

This reading experience was developed by Mark Pearlman's Rethink Partners, an organization dedicated to shifting user and industry perspectives through a combination of business strategy, product management, sales and marketing, editorial, design and online implementation.

Rethink Partners works with for-profit and non-profit organizations to help them reach their potential. We are focused on seeing both what is and what could be.

Visit us at www.rethinkpartners.com.

Acknowledgements

This book would not have been possible without the help of many people. Special thanks goes to:

Mark Pearlman, for documenting the Rabbi Pinson and other world-class teachings on video over the past decade, for helping hundreds of thousands of people access these lectures in events and on the Internet through Sinai Live and JInsider, and for his initiative to create and publish this unique book.

Jake Laub, for his creativity in design and diligence in editing.

Raquel Amram, for her meticulous transcriptions and editing.

Daniel Schanler, for his expertise in video editing and production.

Made in United States
North Haven, CT
26 November 2023

44571792R00035